For Ann

with best wishes,

Alison

Possibly a Pomegranate

Palewell Press

Possibly a Pomegranate

Poems – Alwyn Marriage

Possibly a Pomegranate

First edition 2022 from Palewell Press,
www.palewellpress.co.uk

Printed and bound in the UK

ISBN 978-1-911587-61-3

Acknowledgements

Poems in this collection have already appeared in:

Saturday's Child - *Touching Earth*, 2007
Skin - *Touching Earth*, 2007
Nancy's star turn - Shortlisted, *Poetry on the Lake competition*, 2016; published in *Project Boast*, 2018
Ski Scene - 1st published in *festo: Celebrating winter & Christmas*, 2012
Schoolgirl, Bolivia - *Dedalus*, 2016
Six impossible things before breakfast - *The Alice in Wonderland Anthology, 2015*
Cherry Orchard - Jo Bell's *Guardian page*: challenge on archaeology; 1st prize *BigUp competition*
Moving on - *Poems for a Liminal Age*, 2015
La Matelote - *French Literary Review*, 2010; *Artemis*, 2011
Women's literacy class - *The Selkie, Winter,* 2019
Paying the Price - *I am not a silent poet*, 2015; published in *Art Saves Lives International*
Primrose Time - *Writers' Café issue 5; Love and music,* February 2018
Island Gifts – *The Wild Words*, Spring 2022
Late Home - *PK on line,* 2021
Possibly a pomegranate - *Acumen*, 2018
Bikini - *Pop Up Anthology* 2013; *Touching earth*, 2007
Veiled - *Poetry on the Lake, Crossing Borders*, 2017
Finger Four – *Dreich*, 2020
Newspaper picture - *New International Times,* Spring 2020
Produce of the earth - *Writers' Café. Elements*, 2018
Speculate - *Pandora's Pandemic,* 2021
Same person? - *Pandora's Pandemic,* 2021
Menses - *Acumen*, 2007; *Touching Earth*, 2007; *Bloody Amazing, 2020*
Conversation with magic stones - *Wordstrokes: The poetry of art*, 2016

Silver threads - *Agenda, Ekphrastic issue* 2019
The clue lies in the lady's toe - Winner in *Bedford Open Poetry Competition*, 2011; Published in *The Interpreter's House*, 2012
Couple arm in arm - *Sarasvati,* February 2018
Childproof - *Seven ages of Woman*, 2016
Clapper boards - Commended in *PS Stanza competition* 2014; published on *National Poetry Day website*
Losing It - *The Interpreter's House*, 2011
Lost Scents - *Book of Love and Loss*, ed RV Bailey & June Hall, 2014
GPS - *Notes from a camper van*, 2014; *Poetry Space Autumn Showcase*, 2015
Water Music - *Broadsheet*, October 2016; *Writers' Café Issue 5, 'Love and music'*, on-line February 2018
Venus of Willendorf - *Artemis, 2021*
Her Lot - Highly commended in *Poetry on the Lake competition*, 2015; *Blue Nib Literary Magazine,* 2020.
Far Outpost - *Wild Court*, 2021
Sic et Non - *In the Image, IDP,* 2017
Hildegard: Doctor of the Church - *Hildegard: visions & inspiration*, Wyvern Works Limited Edition, 2014; *Women's Literary Culture and the Mediaeval Canon*, June 2016; Displayed in Winchester Cathedral at the *Ten Days Arts Festival*, 2015; *In the Image, IDP* 2017
Mother Julian and the Astronauts - *In the Image, IDP,* 2017
Edward mourns for Eleanor - *In the Image, IDP,* 2017
Jane Austen's tombstone - *Advice on Proposals*, 2014
Point of Grace – *Sarasvati* 2018
RP RIP - *Project Boast*, 2017; winner of the Leeds Peace Poetry Prize, 2015
Pebbles at Hallsands, *Acumen* 2020
Whale - *Domestic Cherry,* 2013; *Artemis*, Autumn 2015; *Six British Poets*, Romania, 2016

My thanks to Camilla Reeve, Senior Editor at Palewell Press, who has been a delight to work with on this collection.

For Phoebe, Rhona and Freya, with love.

Contents

SOMEWHERE A CHILD...

Saturday's child

I stretch into the morning, waking late.
Already, birds are weaving skeins of song between the trees,
sunlight blinking spots of grass alight.

Somewhere a child leaps from bed, remembering
just in time to open eyes before
tumbling into morning.

Dozing, an old woman tries to shift position; wracked
with pain she rolls and groans, surprised, and none too pleased
to see another day.

Two lovers smell each other's bodies in their dreams,
nestle close, anticipate
fresh hours of exploration and delight.

A man who lost respect, income and hope
yesterday when work and world came to an end,
is caught for a moment in the normal joy of waking,

before memory clicks into the ratchet of
despair again, reality readjusts itself,
darkness returns.

Around the world, soldiers fight;
young mothers offer breasts to infants, feel
their life force flow; pacts and truces

are made and tried and tested; flowers and ferns
uncurl. And as I stir
I feel the first faint flutter in my womb.

Skin

Phoebe

Light shines through
the package in ultra-thin covering
snuggling on my knee.

Firm, plump, soft, embracing
the perfume of a fig that's ripe for eating:
I bury my nose to inhale your sweetness.

Leaning against my breast
and dreaming down the years,
your small, strong fingers fondle mine,

discovering and pulling at
the folds of loose flesh on my hands
that surprise me, unite me

with generations of incredulous women
who learned from the wisdom of their grandchildren
that they were on their way to growing old.

Nancy's star turn

We were five years old, newly-fledged to school
shy, except for one girl with pretty yellow curls

who spoke loudly and cheerfully in a strange
accent, didn't defer to teachers or avoid the boys,

but when we gathered to drink our third of a pint
of milk at break time, climbed onto a desk

(it wasn't even her desk), and raising her squeaky
voice in a shrill rendering of *Nelly the Elephant*,

proceeded to click and tap the heels
of her impossibly shiny patent leather shoes

in a dance whose fierce percussive beat
thrilled our innocence, suggesting there were worlds

wider and more exciting than our own,
of which Nancy knew but we could only dream.

The cruelty of schoolgirls

Little things can sometimes fan the flames,
like calling people *Gormless*, *Looney* or *Titch*.
I'm sorry that I used to call you names.
I didn't think, but joined the others' games
in a web of relationships formed on the hockey pitch
where little things can sometimes fan the flames.
We weren't intentionally cruel in our aims
and *Titch* was meant to be affectionate, though kitch;
but I'm sorry that I used to call you names.
Gormless, the glasses you wore had thick pink frames
and there were whispers that your mother was a witch.
Little things can sometimes fan the flames   .
We mocked you, *Looney,* for your far-fetched claims
that your brother was a pop-star and your father rich,
but I'm sorry that I used to call you names   .
The memory of what you must have suffered shames
me into realising I was a schoolgirl bitch.
Little things can sometimes fan the flames
so I'm sorry that I used to call you names.

Ski scene

Controlling fear, contracting muscles, I wind
down curving piste while trying not to see
the plummeting depth below. I have to find
both strength and courage, so that I can ski.

As I reach the bottom, a young girl joins the queue
before me for the lift. Unfit and overweight, she's
childishly dependent, out of place. I view
her mother help her hold the bar and point her skis.

Dragged back up to the dizzying height, I see
the girl stand close behind her mother, free her hand
then fearlessly follow her down the slope ahead of me.
My eyes are suddenly opened, and I understand:

Trusting the mother and skiing fast behind
requires great courage, for the child is blind.

Schoolgirl, Bolivia

high on the altiplano
you follow a donkey track
barefoot, carrying tucked
under your arm, a book

when you are older
you'll wear a bowler hat
drink coca tea, have babies
cook corn in an old clay pot

remember how you used to walk
ten miles to school and back,
and the soft sweet smell left behind
by pack animals trudging the path

ahead of you in bright clear air,
a vulture circling overhead
and a cactus flowering
once in a hundred years

Petticoat

Having worn glasses all his life
he appeared naked, vulnerable
when he took them off

but to my childhood eyes,
there was something strange
and exciting about the way

he bent to gently lift my mother's
skirt and wipe his lenses
on her soft white petticoat.

Such casual intimacy every day
always reassured me, suggesting
he was still in love with her,

but years later this tender
dependence was forgotten,
her petticoat no longer worn.

All change

Both parents were there, dressed
to the nines, my father
looking like a character
from Trollope.

I could see that amazing picture
of the shipwreck of St Paul,
with flickering lights bringing
the vibrant colours to life

and from the corner of my eye
I saw so many friends and relatives
I hadn't seen for years, all smiling
at me, wishing me well

and very soon the feast
was revealed, wine began
to flow, chatter to increase
in volume

and maybe I knew, and maybe
I didn't, that nothing would ever
be quite the same
again.

Rendezvous

sleep-drugged, my limbs
slowly respond to a lost voice
summoning me through space,

wailing through
the echoing bright darkness
of the milky way

I lift your sadness
to my body, catch
my breath in pleasure

as I feel you latch
onto your docking station,
go with the flow.

Cherry Orchard

This patch was clearly once a small town garden,
perched on a chalk ridge of the Surrey downs
and enjoying the advantage of a southerly aspect.

The garden was contained within a boundary stone wall,
the shape and size of which can still be traced
from the flint and rubble that surround the plot.

Rusted remains of a cooker and some fragments
of a small domestic 'fridge suggest a modest dwelling
of a type quite common at the start of this millennium.

Various species of grass and copious dandelions
now smother the past in shades of gold and green,
so that what might have been is hidden;

and over all, a waving froth of pink
startles a blue Spring sky,
promising a fruitful future and providing evidence,

if it were needed, that at least one person
on a number of occasions in summers long ago,
sat in this garden spitting cherry stones.

Six impossible things before breakfast

Like what?
demanded Alice.
Well ... the white queen hesitated
trying to formulate something
that was obviously impossible
but that she could imagine, (ignorant
of the fact that a number of philosophers
have grappled with this problem
over the years).

Then, grasping each finger in turn
as she enumerated, she began:

*1. I expect you think that when the sun
goes down, no one can read a book,
because the light from oil lamps and from
candles is too dim. But I manage to believe
that everyone could flick a little switch
that would instantly illuminate
all the rooms within their house,
making night as bright as day.*

*2. With a little more effort
it's possible to believe
that you and I could be
transported at enormous speed
to Timbuktu and back
without the aid of horse
and carriage.*

*3. It's possible, you know,
to keep a tiny pet machine
on which to imprint messages
that can be simultaneously read*

on the far side of the world
(if anyone there happens to be sitting
at their desk, rather than slumbering
in bed).

4. If I try hard enough
I can even believe it's possible
 to send a strange-shaped vehicle
into outer space
and land it accurately on a comet
over two hundred and sixty
million miles away.

5. I stubbornly believe
 that countries that go to war,
slay millions of each other's citizens,
lay waste to the most beautiful cities,
breed distrust and engender hate,
can, within a few short years,
learn to respect each other and join
in a peaceful union of nations.

6. And this morning I even believed
that a little girl could pass through glass
into my realm, and then expect
to get away without losing her head.

Alice gave the queen a quizzical look,
and as she plotted her escape
(hoping, rather than believing,
that it was possible), decided
that if she ever made it back
to normal life, instead of daydreaming
she'd study science and engineering.

Field trip

Lie down, he said, which admittedly
was a rather strange instruction
for a biology master to give,
even on a field trip.

Look up. So twenty giggly girls
did as we were told, and gazed
at the interlacing boughs and
twigs of the ancient beech tree.

Silence embraced us. *This
is the best cathedral you will
ever visit*, he continued. *Don't
waste your time travelling the world*

*but come out here, lie down
and worship. Today you can
enjoy the shapes in blue, which
tomorrow may be grey or white,*

*while tonight the twigs will decorate
a roof that's spangled with stars. Look,
and now look even further, deeper
into space; lose yourself and be found.*

*When you are sheltering in stuffy rooms,
remember this sacred space in which
even then, a blanket will be letting down
healing waters to welcome growth.*

I forgot to giggle, failed to notice
the discomfort of husks of mast
that were embedding themselves
into my back.

I didn't do well in that term's biology
exam, but discovered in the green heart
of the woods, where tree top and sky meet
to dance, a way into the mystery of life.

Moving on

The first time I heard you speak of *home*,
not meaning the house where I live
and where you'd spent your childhood,
there was a slight, but perceptible
shuddering in my foundations.

Flesh from my flesh, ever since your journey
started I had been letting go;
but feared this visible and physical
realignment to our world
might lead to the final separation.

Time proved the opposite; but for a while
I had to watch while you learnt to adjust
to life in a place you didn't know, while I,
just as tentatively, grew accustomed
to a home empty of you.

PRIMROSE TIME

Artist, mid-morning

Tracy Emin

Make your bed,
her mother said;
you're a disgrace
and this whole place
looks just like a slum.

Tracy glanced at her rumpled bed
with the eye of a creator,
and resolved that if
forced to make it now,
she'd get her own back later.

The unkindest cut

Fairy mops

several times a year we paired up in my kitchen,
or in the garden if the sun was shining,
to cut each other's hair

my long locks needed just a straightening trim
while your wild mop of curls required more care
and patience.

as our conversation grew more animated
and we shared the intimate secrets of our hearts,
scissors flew faster, cuts deeper, hair moved north

until the day you made the final cut,
severing ties with husband, neighbours, friends,
and moved away beyond our reach for ever

for many years my hair kept growing longer
but, unlike Samson, that didn't make me stronger.

Aware

— of air
still when I am still
moving when
my body moves

— of forest floor
deep pile of leaves
echoed here
in carpet, soft
receptacle for feet

— of this mysterious
collection of particles
translated into skin and bones,
warm flesh and hair
that's open to everything
that surrounds me,
that is in me
that is me
breathing a world
into existence

— and in spite of pain
within, without,
I see and feel
that it is good.

La Matelote

the restaurant was called *la Matelote*,
– the same word as *le matelot*
but ending in an 'e'
and therefore feminine.

We debated what a female sailor
would be called in English
other than, of course,
a sailor –

fish wife hasn't quite the same
éclat: shore-bound and down-to-earth,
she scolds her husband
wipes scale-covered hands on bloodied apron;

sailor girl sounds
far more jaunty, even saucy,
a jolly sea shanty of a lass
who's good at knots, but lacks maturity;

a *woman of the waves*, though cumbersome,
has a more romantic ring,
laid-back and offering
her ebb and flow, her undulating curves.

In our minds these women all
transmogrified into a mermaid,
sea-born and always breaking free
like words for which there's no equivalent.

Consulting a dictionary to check
the latest addition to our French vocabulary
we found 'la matelote'
simply means *fish stew*.

Women's literacy class

Bangladesh

After travelling deep into the paddy
on a rickshaw, we balanced on a strip
of dry bank between two flooded rice fields,
to cover the final kilometre on foot.

Ten teenaged village girls had been away
to receive three weeks of basic training
in how to read and write and how to teach,
before returning to share their expertise.

We sat on bare ground, chickens pecking among us,
as gradually the corners of saris covering shy faces
dropped away, along with the darkness of ignorance,
revealing new-found confidence and hope.

At the back, beyond the circle of light, the men stood in a ring
looking nonchalant, gazing at their feet,   secretly listening.

Paying the price

She used to have an elder sister and a brother,
but now there's no one left to help her
collect the wood and light a fire.

After the man spoke with the village elders
he came to see her sister, test the flesh,
assess her strength and beauty,

and though she wouldn't raise her eyes to see
the visitor, he inspected all her other features
and deemed her worth the price.

There was no choice, no opportunity to exercise
her filial duty, or rebel; the price was paid
and he departed with his goods. The sale

provided money for her brother's fees
at school, until the army came and took
the boy away to train in arts of war.

The money's all been spent, the precious
children gone, leaving only a father's shame,
a mother's grief and a lonely child.

Thai dancing class

Watch what I do
Music slinks into the room
and twenty multicoloured
chakkri form a moving circle,
arms waving, bodies swaying,
hands tracing intricate patterns
above shining black heads.
> *I listen to the music*
> *watch carefully*
> *and wait.*

Follow me
The music doesn't pause,
as twenty western hopefuls
take to the floor, each
shadowing a dancer,
start to absorb the music,
patiently, painstakingly
copying each graceful gesture.
> *I begin to feel*
> *the music,*
> *try to imitate.*

You're on your own
The patterns we've been
following slip away
to the edges of the room
where they can watch,
smiling encouragement,

as we breathe the rhythm
let it flow through limbs
to decorate the air around us
>*No instruction has*
>*been given, but slowly,*
>*slightly stiffly, I am*
>*responding to the music,*
>*and becoming the dance.*

Exploration

Pitch black. Are you still there
or have you gone downstairs?

If I reach out towards you
with my hand, you'll wake

and arousal will put paid
to the possibility of sleep

so I edge my foot towards
your side of the bed

and my toes purr as they
touch bare skin.

Primrose time

I wake, your left hand
cupped round my right breast,
your breath stroking my cheek

it's primrose time
pale yellow sunshine
seeps under my eyelids
finds a smile
and plants it gently
on your lips.

High wire

a line   stretched tight   high above   what looks like   endless
darkness

years of training
have brought me here
to show the crowd below
that gravity holds
no terrors for me
       as a child, balancing
       on school bench upside-
       down, acting the clown
       on a low wall, then
       climbing higher, laughing
       at the upturned faces
       of the earth-bound
              later, the comfort
              of a safety net
              unseen in the pit
              but still the basis
              of belief, helping me
              to overcome my fear
                     no room for doubt now
                     on this narrow wire
                     which I must cross
                     knowing that if
                     I put a foot wrong

                       I must
                            fly
                                  or
                                     die

Island gifts

Tossing about on board the first boat
of the season to set a northerly course
towards the rocks of Staffa,
you hinted at the loneliness
of your orientation.

Later, on the beach,
you showed me the smooth
green stones they call
Columba's tears,
selected a perfect one
and placed it gently in my palm.

As evening shadows deepened
you celebrated our new-found friendship
by inviting me to the ancient unfrequented
chapel behind the abbey, where you sang
Mary's lullaby just for me, your clear sweet
tenor voice chiming with Celtic cadences
as it stroked the stones, sanctifying the space
and rising to join the astonished choirs of angels.

When you finished,
the soft reverberations
still held us in the silence
of deep, loving reverence
and gratitude for a gift
that would continue to be
treasured through the years.

Triple relief

You tumble through the front door,
desperate to kick your shoes off
with abandon, but find you can't
because the pavements of the town
have ingrained their contours
deep into the unfit of your feet,
and so, with help from hands
and winkling toe to heel, you

                              e a s e

them off.

Moving up the stairs to change
your clothes, remove the imprint
of the outer world, you pause,
anticipate then experience
the sheer relief as your body
is released from the bullying bra;
and maybe it was worth being
held by it all day, just to relish
that moment; and as your breasts
break bud to blossom, and you

                              e x p a n d

you wonder if there is any
equivalent delight for men.

Much later, sitting up in bed,
leaning back and balancing
against the pillows, reading,
writing, talking until exhaustion
overcomes your desire to extend
the day and you slip, naked,
down under the duvet, exhale
as you are welcomed into
soft sleep-inducing comfort,
body sinking earthward,
pillow cossetting heavy head,
every particle of your body
exulting in this final day-ending

s t r e

t

c

h.

Late home

Midnight in South London
and the last suburban
train spills out

the artless attractiveness
of youth, inviting danger
or at least unwelcome attention

during that final unavoidable
solo mile through darkness
from the station

where kerb-crawlers
call obscenities and
you learn to minimise

their threat by walking
briskly counter flow
instead of dawdling

checking that no car
is following when you
turn from the main road

into your quiet residential
street where fifty yards ahead
the curtain of a house

is pulled aside, and you see,
with mixed relief and
irritation a pale face

pressed to the window and
you know that by the time
you reach the gate

it will have disappeared
so that when you enter
the safe haven of home

all will be silent, still,
the sense of a mother's
satisfaction, palpable.

Possibly a pomegranate

It makes no sense to speculate
on mundane details of a far-fetched story,
including the nature of the fruit
Eve picked in the Garden of Eden;
myths may appear unreal and playful,
but they present us with the mystery
that our oldest stories sometimes hold
more truth than history.

The closeness of the Latin words
for apple and for evil makes it tempting
to substitute one for the other;
and artists down the ages
have perpetuated the confusion,
giving flesh to the mythical fruit,
and displaying with veracity and tenderness
the juicy plumpness of an apple.

The point is not how many seeds were
in the fruit, how sweet or sour or round
it was, but what explanation the creative mind
of generations could come up with to account
for the way things are: the hubris of humanity,
our meddlesome nature, our inability
to live at peace in paradise
and our capacity for choosing evil.

But if we take the story at face value,
it may, indeed, have been an apple,
or possibly a pomegranate.

In Latin, malum *means evil,* malus *is an apple tree
and* malum *is an apple.*

WOMAN IN THE MIRROR

Bikini

Pacific blue, my old bikini rises from the drawer,
shedding the somnolence of two decades
in which a series of more sober swimming costumes
wiggled down the catwalk of my holidays.

The question then, as I stood sideways to the mirror,
was whether my delicately curving stomach appeared
concave or convex. A test no longer needed,
sadly, but superseded by new challenges.

No cheating, no tightening
of muscles, holding breath
or pulling stomach in.
All will be revealed, I squeeze
new wine-fed flesh
into old wine skin,

wondering whether a periscope is needed
for looking in a southerly direction. Can
Mons Venus still be seen
– discreetly covered in my blue bikini;
or is the view of pubic hair impeded?

Veiled

Hijab

If I veiled
would you know me
or pass me unsuspecting
in a crowd?

Chador

Will you see below
the colour of my skin: the shape
of nose, or curve that catches
smiles born in my eyes?

Burka

A fleeting image of a woman, shrouded,
scuttling out of the side of a television screen.

In the foreground men, burning books
burning flags, burning with rage.

Niqab

A London street,
miles of cultural alienation
from the place called home.

I smile at you
and in return receive
a miracle of veiled communication.

Finger four

Away from home and parents,
fifteen years old and starry-eyed,
I was taken fishing in a rowing boat,
by Jimmy on the Clyde.

We were singing *James, James,*
hold the ladder steady when the hook
on his line flew in my direction,
catching the edge of my left hand's
fourth finger and drawing blood.

It didn't hurt much, but left a little scar
that failed to fade entirely even when
that holiday romance and all my memories
of Jimmy were overlaid, and someone else,
just a few years later slipped a ring
onto that finger.

After nearly half a century
of wear and tear and faithfulness
the gold still shines today;
but even now, if I remove my wedding ring,
I find a faint reminder of a Scottish boy
who, though he sang so sweetly on a sunny day,
failed to catch any fish, or me.

Risk and refuge

Would I still have done it if I'd known —
not feared or fantasized but fully realised
the dangers I'd encounter on the road?

There was no way I could anticipate
the trudging miles; the loss of dignity
in begging lifts from men I didn't know;
the terrifying claustrophobia
of being squeezed into a stinking lorry;
the panic when my daughter disappeared;
the sentence of perpetual poverty
after I was robbed; the utter loneliness
of my arrival where I was not wanted;
the horror when I became a number,
not a name.

As I cry myself to sleep
I sometimes wonder if I should have stayed;
but then the memories return to haunt my waking
and my dreams: the bombs that rained down
on our street, the darkness when electric power
cut out; the hunger, and worst of all the thirst:
the craving for a tiny drop of water,
while knowing that if I drank, contamination
of supply would lead to days of sickness
followed by painful death.

Re-living in my tortured mind the carnage
and catastrophe, I recognise that getting out
was not just our best option, but more critically,
the last chance possible, our one and only hope.

Newspaper picture

Please don't show me another picture
of an anguished mother weeping for her child.

I already know what grief feels like, and how
most of us look when overwhelmed by tears,

so I'd rather you didn't publicise her raw emotion
which you can't feel and isn't yours to share.

You really haven't any right to splash
this image over the newspaper's front page.

You can share the story by all means, but keep
the prying eyes of photojournalists at bay.

Just let this unhappy woman retain her dignity,
and live to recover from the pain she feels today.

True courage

Surprised in earlier days
to find yourself falling
so deeply in love, you let
your imagination run wild
with possibilities for showing
how much you'd do for him.

You fantasised about
dashing into a burning house,
leaping off a cliff because
he couldn't swim, or jumping
onto his knife-bearing attacker
from behind.

Little did you think
so much *more* courage
would be required of you
to pass your days and nights
for twenty years, patiently
attending to him as his mind
rotted away.

Produce of the earth

I loved you at the crematorium
as the flowers on your wicker coffin
were committed with your body
and our tears into the flames.

I loved you when you dug
vegetables from the garden, washed
away the dirt and cooked them for
your hungry family.

I loved you when you leant across
the fence to share your knowledge
and the surplus from another harvest
with our neighbour.

But most of all I loved you when
after hours of digging, you stretched towards
the sun, then bent again and dipped your fingers
back into the soil to plant another seed.

Through your life and death I learnt
to trust the goodness of the earth,
the cycles of the year, your daily care
and the fruits of all your labour.

Speculate

Is that woman in the mirror really me?
I touch the cold hard surface with my hand,
watch fingertips reflecting fingers meeting mine
as the light of truth betrays my fantasies, and
presents an image that I didn't want to see.

I know that my reflection in the glass
is an honest record of how I generally appear:
white hair, pale skin, no longer in my prime;
though how youth disappeared so quickly isn't clear,
it's obvious that all I loved and valued had to pass.

ıııııııııııııı

It's obvious that all I loved and valued had to pass,
though how youth disappeared so quickly isn't clear.
White hair, pale skin, no longer in my prime –
is an honest record of how I generally appear.

I know that my reflection in the glass
presents an image that I didn't want to see.
As the light of truth betrays my fantasies, and
I watch fingertips reflecting fingers meeting mine.
I touch the cold hard surface with my hand.
Is that woman in the mirror really me?

Same person?

following covid

It's too depressing to look at these
two photos side by side,
taken just a year apart but separated
by our modern plague. The first
shows rosy cheeks and glow of health,
while this more recent one presents
a pale ghost damaged by the toll
of illness and advancing years.
I suppose I shouldn't be concerned
with outward appearances, but as
the ravages of coronavirus recede
into the past, I can't help hoping
my looks will recover enough for me
to recognise the woman I used to be.

A house full of emptiness

You were out
when I got home,
the house and garden
empty, silence seeping
out from every corner.

I picked a ripe fig, sat
and ate it on the lawn,
thinking *this is what it would be like
if I lived alone.*

No one to consider, less
shared love and laughter,
no one to make dinner for
or welcome into bed.

I wonder idly where you are,
resolve to show you when you reach
the door how pleased I am
to see you.

Menses

I bleed, and from my body
flows a stream
uniting me with all that's
fruitful in the earth.

I swell, and celebrate
the ripening corn, the apple
and the yeast which multiplies
the cells, sustaining life.

I feel
the rhythm of the tides
which rise and fall and draw
all waters to the sea.

And deep within my body
a lake reflects the glow that lights the night,
mirroring the moon,
pure centre of the rhythm that I share.

The catalogue

A catalogue arrived, uninvited
on my front door mat today

full of photographs of fashionable garments
I would never have been able to afford,

modelled gracefully by elegant women
of a pleasing variety of colours:

such beautiful clothes, including smart
work outfits (which covid has rendered

unnecessary), seductive night clothes
which aren't quite as tempting as

bare flesh, beach wear that would not
survive the breast stroke, let alone

the crawl, and best of all, a range
of gorgeous floaty dresses.

I can just see myself in that one,
and this other lovely creation

which in the absence of a catwalk
I could wear to flounce around at home,

until I notice that all the models
wearing them are under-nourished,

that the slinky materials hang softly
and evenly with no bumps and bulges

and that they are all at least thirty years
younger than, I now remember, I am.

Conversation with magic stones

Barbara Hepworth

a sculptor dancing round her strange
creation, or a dancer giving solid form
to dreams, engages in a conversation,

has a tendency to scatter magic dust,
convincing us, against the evidence,
that these bronze shapes are stones;

that one is three, two groups of three
can sometimes become one, and triplets
may be born from one warm womb;

that inanimate figures standing tall,
and multifaceted crouching forms
can somehow become animate

playing an equal part in conversation
between the sculptor and her work,
between her work and those of us

who, against our normal expectations,
watch transfixed by an artist's wizardry
as the stones begin to dance.

Come sun or rain, come
shade or shine, come
shadows playing

over moss, in mist, against
the backdrop of a vast infinity
of sky the dance goes on.

Are the magic stones transformed
into each other? Or am I transformed
by my conversation with them?

Silver threads

You're older now than I was
when the colour of my hair
began to fade

you're slimmer, fitter, faster
than I am, relishing the power
of youth, still in your prime

it's becoming difficult to hold
the winding threads of history
as years multiply

and slithers of silver
start to weave mysteriously
through your dark hair

CRISS-CROSS THE LABYRINTH

The clue lies in the lady's toe

On visiting Henry Moore's sculpture in Dumfries and Galloway

On a Scottish hillside the bronze statue
of an archetypal king and queen
braves the elements,

observing, perhaps, a thread
of slit-eyed sheep winding up the hill,
with careful, delicate tread,

yellow marks like lichen
on their rumps, their gaze
full of vague unanswered questions.

My mind, also, struggles to explain
the different texture of the metal on
the king's right knee. While all the rest

is stippled, rippled, riven
in a pattern to catch the varying
shades of light, his knee is smooth.

What point was the sculptor making
as he carefully fashioned this
one unblemished surface?

Only as I descend the hill
does a clear-cut memory emerge
from long ago, as I recall

a constant stream of pilgrims
filing past a marble statue of
the queen of heaven,

the slight roughness of the stone
contrasting sharply with the smooth
and shining toe

which generations of the pious
have knelt to fondle and to kiss,
wearing away the awkward corners

and bringing out a deeper shine. The line
of sheep has reached the sculpture now,
and as I watch

each sidles up to the impassive king
and meditatively rubs her rump
against his knee.

Ageing gracefully

She was old, bedridden, two-thirds blind

but instead of growing into a crinkled crone
as she shrank, she came to resemble
a silver fairy.

I know this, because
I used to sit beside her
on the bed
brushing her hair.

Hair history

soft fontanel fuzz
flowered slowly into golden curls,
taking temporary advantage
of that short age of cuteness
in which so many adults
form the wrong assumption
that a pretty little girl
is likely to be good

then locks grew wild, unruly,
as a multitude of thoughts
tumbled over one another
in teenaged intellectual rage,
which only gradually distilled
into philosophy

with approaching adulthood
the (delicious) realisation dawned
that these long thick chestnut
tresses could be partially tamed
while still preserving enough
of the unpredictable to catch
unwary males

and now, even now, to my surprise,
people sometimes stop to look
at hair which has resisted faded brown
or grey, and unapologetically billows
in exuberant and shining white.

Couple arm in arm

Young and newly-forged
in love, they couldn't bear
to be apart, clung as close
in walking as in sleeping,
oblivious to worlds beyond
the entwining of their shared
proximity, electric currents
sparking back and forth
between them.

Fifty years of faithfulness
have flown, and now,
still walking arm in arm,
they tenderly but surreptitiously
support each other, she a bird
in his branches, he the wine
in her cup.

Respice finem

Look to the end (my school motto)

We did —
not aiming high
to plot the route
by which we might arrive
at the ambitious heights
expected of us,
but ticking off the days
until we could get out,
choose our own path
and exercise our freedom.

Later, as my body swelled
with promise of new life,
the best way to survive
the discomfort and indignity
was to believe that there would be
an end to pregnancy, the start
of life for a new person
and for me.

But as old age begins
its insidious decline
towards what we all know
must be the end of ends,
we hold each day as dear,
look back along the path
we've travelled, try not to notice
that the finishing line is near.

Diana

I only met you once, but every year
the letter with your husband's Christmas card
brings cheer, by making me believe
in human love again.

Even now your hair, he says,
is silky, shiny, frames the familiar face.
You smile, your eyes light up. Sometimes your words
come in a recognisable order, almost sound

as though they might make sense.
You walk together down the same old paths;
criss-cross the labyrinth of the autumn park
to the same bench; eat another ice cream, raise

your faces to the sun. Your homely presence
reassures him, makes him think, believe
or simply hope you know him,
that these rituals bring you pleasure.

Childproof

She'd survived her husband and all but one
of her younger brothers and sisters,
borne the pains of childbirth,
discovered through redundancy
what it meant to be idle, unimportant,
coped with the loneliness of widowhood,
managed on a meagre pension,
felt her separation from distant children,
remembered her friends' birthdays and anniversaries,
and filled her loneliness with small deeds of kindness.
In other words, she'd lived.
But what finally drove her to distraction,
persuaded her that she was old and feeble,
was her inability to open jars and bottles.

Clapper boards

after Cape Cod Morning by Edward Hopper

It took twenty years or more
before the trees gave up their souls
and bodies to the woodcutter.

Summer, autumn, winter and spring
seasoned the sappy wood before
they cut it into boards

to build the house and paint it white,
catching the light which seemed to fall
sideways on her waiting face

as she stood for hours in the place
where she could watch
the ever-empty sea.

Losing it

for Jen

At first it was just
the odd word that he lost,
common words that somehow
slipped from his memory
instead of off his tongue;
and they laughed together
at the worst of these aberrations,
saw them simply as symptoms
of the normal aging process.

Then he mislaid names
of people with whom he was familiar,
became embarrassed, and then ceased to care,
unaware that there would be no cure
for the disappearing past, the gritty palimpsest
wiped clean by his forgetfulness;
until finally the thread of his reality
unravelled in the fog and fury
that was closing in on him.

He lost his job, could not remember
why it ever mattered. Then,
because they could no longer cope
with gardening, bills and all the rest,
they sold the house
that they had bought together and in which
their family had grown and flown the nest
to become strangers to him.

It wasn't long before she realised
that though she still lived with a man
who looked like him,
she had lost her husband.

Doing a ton

News flew
through thin air
and the occasional
wire to where
I was on holiday
in a high mountain
ski resort.

The taxi driver
didn't hesitate
to guarantee
he'd get me there,
rising to the challenge
as the needle
on the dial hovered
over a hundred miles an hour.

Like a reckless skier
he ignored
or skilfully negotiated
blind corners,
steep descents
and narrow passes.

I caught the plane
with only seconds
to spare,
sat staring down
at where I'd been
just hours before
on unspoilt snow,

slept, woke
for landing,

was hurried through
formalities to the
waiting car
that drove as fast
as heavy traffic allowed
to the hospital, light
fading with my hope,
as I arrived
too late.

Un-naming

A friend's mother, in residential care,
reached the great age of 104
before she died,

then passed over peacefully
in her sleep, as though just moving
into an adjacent room.

My friend had faith, believed
her mother's death was not the end
and let her go.

But what hurt, what woke her
to the full finality
and released her tears

was removing all the name tags
before disposing of
her mother's clothes.

Lost scents

You saw the badgers just months before you died:
the satisfaction of a long-held dream
caught in our headlights, tumbling down the road;
and though the mellow cuckoo deep within the woods
eluded you, the skein of skylark song
emerged, just once, from background drone
to lift you briefly up in sheer delight.

But you had lost, irrevocably, your sense of smell,
would sniff frustratedly at flowers and lotions
then look around accusingly as though
we hadn't shared a joke.
Nettles and flowering sea beet worked no magic
and even heady hyacinths in spring
couldn't pierce the blank. We wondered
whether aromatherapy might work;
if there was anything that could restore
olfactory satisfaction.

Now the question hinges on belief or fantasy.
Has cessation of your damaged mortal breath
released imprisoned scents?
Is it possible
that joys restored are wafting over you
in a dimension I can no more see
now, than you could smell then.

Morning wear

When you died I kept the full-length
dressing gown you made and wore
each morning in your last ten years of life

the intensity of its rich red velvet
relieved by the white crocheted collar,
that is now unravelling.

After twenty years of daily wear by you
and then by me, the power of its soft caress
on skin is undiminished

and each morning when I slip it over
waking nakedness, my body revels in
your motherly embrace.

Water music

A woman is humming Mozart
in the shower, the splashes
and gushing water woven with
a familiar aria from the Magic Flute.

Her bubble of melody floats up, then bursts
into a sudden silence. Has she forgotten
what notes come next, or has her attention
wandered onto more prosaic matters?

But no, here comes the tune again,
picked up effortlessly in the key
and at the point she would have reached
if she had gone on singing.

Clearly the music continued unabated
internalised while she bent down to soap
her toes, the same song flowing
in and out between her mind and lips.

Is this what happened to Ophelia
when she scattered snatches of old songs?
And as she sang her last and sank to watery death,
did the music travel with her to the other side?

GPS

That other woman in your car
always makes it clear that she knows best:
Continue 5.7 miles on the motorway she orders,
and because there isn't any other option,
you do as she says.

She's bossy and insensitive, lacks sympathy
for your mistakes, shows no respect
for you or for your passengers,
pours scorn on my map-reading
and has never introduced
an interesting topic of conversation
or shown any interest in your life.

In point eight of a mile, keep right
she chimes and, despite your life-long
left-leaning tendencies, you obediently
nose out towards the A road's central lane.

She's clearly got you hooked. Does she enjoy
the power she holds over you? *Continue
20 miles on M5 (or 6 or 20); Perform
a legal U-turn;* or if she's feeling slightly
more polite: *Please drive to highlighted route.*

Amazed, I watch you meekly follow
her directions with no sign of argument
or irritation. I can't believe
the fundamental change I see in you,
and marvel at this new relationship.
You clearly trust a distant satellite
more than you trust your wife.

WINDS OF HISTORY

Sappho

a glose

Tonight I've watched the moon
and then the Pleiades go down ...
The night is now half-gone;
youth goes; I am in bed alone. (Fragment 52)

Last night and every night
since we first met, we slept
together, shared the secrets
of our hearts, discussed
philosophy and poetry.
But now you've left, I swoon
with misery in my empty bed,
knowing you will not come. To learn
how inconstant love can change so soon,
tonight I've watched the moon.

Other loves have come and gone,
lighting up the darkness of my life
like the seven sisters of the midnight sky.
Some I loved for the beauty of their bodies,
while others brought illumination to my mind;
but you alone deserved to be the crown
of my affection. Your brightness lit my way
through misunderstanding and disgrace; but now
I watch the lights extinguished in the town
and then the Pleiades go down.

I drank so deeply at the springs of wisdom,
gave my life and soul to poetry.
Fame came at last, the praise of those
who saw me as a star. I burned and blazed
across the sky; and every night

while others slept, I still wrote on
brightening the world with words.
But now I am eclipsed.
Light fades where once stars shone:
the night is now half-gone.

Nothing is constant; and all too soon
the winds of fortune shake the branches,
sending fragments of papyrus fluttering down
through history. I fear this palimpsest
of poetry is all for which I'll be remembered.
Youth, fame and love have now all flown,
and you have gone. As my star fades and age
creeps up on me, I'm lost. But you, no doubt,
would laugh and say I should have known
youth goes; I am in bed alone.

Venus of Willendorf

Fatty
passion pussy
sexy seed bed
and eternal mother

you don't need me
to write a poem for you
— you are a poem

resonant with meaning,
form and content
in perfect harmony

It's undeniable you're more
shapely than any woman
would choose to be today

but though you're so unlike
me, you tie me to my sisters
down through all the ages

You can't aspire to looking
cool on fashion's catwalk,
or avoid unwelcome attention

but in your full-bellied
full-breasted exuberance
you celebrate fecundity.

Cleopatra's amuse-bouche

Bon appetit Marc Antony,
enjoy my lavish
hospitality.

I feel your gaze
linger where my robe
reveals the smooth round
whiteness of my breast

then rise astonished to
the huge white milky
pendant pearls, best
proof, if it were needed,
of my opulence.

But clearly this is not
enough to win our bet,
for despite the smouldering
passion, you still wear
your Roman smirk
and neither the world's
most precious earrings,
nor this profligate feast
can breach your cold determination
not to be impressed by Egypt's
wealth, or dent your disbelief
that I could spend
ten million sesterces
on one tempting meal.

/continued

I hold your gaze,
know how to mesmerise,
as slowly, slinkily
I unhook one pearl
from where it hangs
below my ear,
waft it in sinuous circles,
to catch the evening light
before submerging it
in the chalice of vinegar.

No one speaks or moves.
The hand you raised
to arrest my action
remains suspended,
as, together, our eyes sink
deep into the liquid.

Slowly, oh so
satisfyingly slowly,
the wealth of pharaohs
is dissolved. It disappears
but is still there,
suspended in both time and space,
awaiting the denouement
of my choice.

I raise the cup
and sup,
savouring the faint taste
of shellfish and of
surf-lined shores
spiced with sharp delight
as I glimpse the horror
on your face.

When my fingers reach again,
you seem to wake and shake
yourself out of a trance,
catch my right hand
and hold it tight
before I can remove
the first pearl's twin.

So, Latin lover,
proud Marc Antony,
tell me: did I win?

Her Lot

Genesis 19

Fleeing a city's devastation with his wife
he was witness to her transformation,
stopped in his tracks aghast, then tentatively
took two steps backwards without turning round.
He spoke to her, gently at first, then cried
with rising panic in his voice,
put out a hand to touch her cold white form,
but withdrew it as he felt the sculpture burn
with the salt tears of strife.

Licking his fingers in disbelief, he briefly savoured
twenty shared years in which she'd added flavour
to his life. Ozymandias in the desert wastes
couldn't have looked more lost and isolated
than this woman he must now leave behind,
as abandoning the strange and yet familiar
column of solidified sea water,
he set his face to the impassivity of rock
and continued on his desert way, without looking back.

Looking back

So much was left behind, of course I felt regret:
that's why I glanced back for one quick last sight.
I'd repeatedly warned my husband not to let
himself be influenced by his guests last night
but as it happened, I was given no say
even when he offered our daughters to the men
instead of the strangers. *Here, have your way
with these young virgins,* he called out; but then
disaster fell on them and on the wicked city
partly as punishment for their attempted rape.
Now I'm paralysed by bitterness and pity
instead of gratitude that we made our escape.
It didn't dawn on me that this was my own fault
until I realised that the bitter taste was salt.

Far Outpost

Vindolanda

Before they built the wall
(in our opinion, in completely
the wrong place)
and marched along it
shouting orders at each other

we tried to reproduce the more refined
and delicate pleasures that we'd left behind
in Italy, only to discover that no wishing wells
could ever produce figs or olives
from these cold English hills.

But you, my sister, knew how to entertain,
offering the food of gossip and the wine
of intelligent conversation, so that for a while
we could forget the weather, the dirt, the wild
brutish ways of men who brought the British mud
into what passed for home,
demanding the same carnal pleasures we'd enjoyed
in the sunshine and soft beds of Rome.

At least it isn't necessary here to flee our homes
in summer, in search of cooling breezes.
Here in this fort, cold winds and driving rain
seek out our bones each day
regardless of the season.

It didn't trouble us that we'd be written out of history.
Our men might punctuate their long dark days
with oaths and curses, skirmishes with local bandits.
We exercised the calligraphic skills
we'd learnt before our exile,

committing to these tablets
words that did not need
to be preserved, but on the other hand
might last two thousand years.
We knew such correspondence
could be used to comfort, offer
culinary and herbal hints
and even to arrange a birthday party.

And so, my sister, friend,
all is not lost
as long as we can write
to one another.
Rome may rise and fall,
history cover all our private
rooms with peat and mud,
but hidden or discovered,
our gentle unimportant words
will last for ever.

Sic et non

Is your name Heloise?
>Yes, that's the name my parents
>gave me at my birth;
>but no, I gave away that name,
>along with my identity,
>when I took the veil.

Did you accept the tutor your uncle chose for you?
>Yes, I was grateful that he understood
>my restless spirit and my need for learning
>to challenge and control my wayward spirit;
>but I was nervous that his choice might be
>a subtle way in which to clip my wings,
>effectively control me.

Was it necessary that you should study Greek and Latin?
>Yes, to understand the Scriptures, stimulate
>my God-given brain; but no,
>I admit that these are not the skills I use in daily life
>or texts I need to know.

Did you find the young philosopher attractive?
>No, at first I was fascinated only by his mind,
>his breadth of knowledge and scholarship
>of a kind I hadn't met before.
>Then yes, oh yes: he set my heart on fire.

Did you both concentrate on conjugations and declensions?
>Yes, we concentrated on the joys of conjugal love.
>And no, in time I did not decline his advances.

Did Abelard take advantage of your innocence?
> Yes, perhaps he was the first to read
> and then translate the stirrings
> that swept us both along;
> But no, strictly he did not seduce me,
> rather he gave me a wide vocabulary
> of Greek and Latin words and guided
> my first clumsy efforts at fitting them
> together to produce sound sense.
> He gave me words I lacked
> to describe and celebrate
> the human anatomy,
> and when I'd mastered those
> he delved still deeper
> into his store of words,
> into my secret chambers.

Were lust and fornication the result of educating a young woman?
> Yes, they followed as night follows day, but
> no, if the blood had not coursed
> so fast and free through our young veins,
> it might then have been different.

Do you regret what happened? confess that you have sinned? accept the punishment you both endured?
> Yes, I know the rules, and do admit
> I broke them; and though I can't repent
> of my love for Abelard, I do, of course, regret
> what followed after, when I lost both love
> and freedom. But no, I will not lament
> the fact that for a time he gave me
> more love and freedom than I'd ever known
> before, or will again.

/continued

*Have you maintained contact with the sinner since he entered
the monastic life?*
> Yes, we correspond by letter; mine
> full of pain and passion, his
> curiously cold and factual.
> No, we do not truly reach each other
> in this way, for neither of us finds it possible
> to communicate what we long to say.

*Have you found contentment in following the will of God and of
the Church?*
> Yes, day follows day according to
> a simple pattern that leaves no need
> or inclination to think;
> but no, contentment has fled away
> for ever, and will not now be found
> within the cloister.

Do you still believe in the power of love?
> Yes, my love has not diminished or abated
> despite the cruel treatment my man of God received.
> But no, it seems the love we thought was strong enough
> to rend the gates of heaven and hell,
> failed to protect us and inevitably fell
> when it met the fury of the clergy.

*'Sic et non', 'Yes and no', is the name of the treatise by the
mediaeval philosopher, Peter Abelard.*

of Bingen

Hildegard: Doctor of the Church

Hildegard believed that herbs for the body's healing
had a part to play, with prayer, in the soul's salvation;
and perceiving the greening of earth and heaven
from far beyond our human understanding,
she celebrated Viriditas, the force that flows
through all that's green and good, in all that grows.

Like many other women since,
she posed a challenge to the Church,
displaying a deep learning never found
in books the clergy knew,
communicated in an alphabet they couldn't read,
and if they could, they wouldn't understand.

Down the centuries we hear her songs of glory
soaring higher in ripieno praise,
above the black-clad choir stalls
and dusty academic libraries
of those who failed to grasp that wisdom
could be grounded in a woman's native wit.

As she joins the other doctors of the Church:
Térèse, Theresa, Catherine of Sienna,
along with sundry men, the question hovers:
will those without a voice today
nine hundred years from now be heard,
admired?

Mother Julian and the Astronauts

To land that seminal image of a tiny
blue ball spinning in the immensity of space,
modern astronauts had to study
physics, technology and mathematics
to develop a craft that could defy
the out-of-bounds beyond earth's atmosphere,
while simultaneously learning how to seal
in a mechanical light box all that the eye revealed.

More than six hundred years ago
a woman who had seen no further
than the four walls of her cell
was moved to describe this fragile sphere
as a hazel nut held in the palm of a hand,
secure and treasured there.

Edward mourns for Eleanor

Eleanor of Castile, 1241-1290

Despite her tender years, she was my chosen bride,
although you never welcomed her. She bore me offspring
and gave you a royal heir, but was painfully aware
of your rejection and dislike. It's rare for a marriage
of convenience to bring such happiness and love,
but she and I were blessed in our relationship.
She joined me on the Eighth Crusade and so was there
to tend my wounds; she made my house and garden
beautiful, enriched not only me but the whole nation
with her love of poetry and song. By night she lay
within my arms, by day she entertained me as we shared
talk and laughter. Would she laugh now to see my tears
and the dozen crosses I've had fashioned out of stone
to trace the route her body took on her last journey home?

Truth or fiction?

If the human imagination
can transfer a walrus horn
onto the forehead of a horse
to create a unicorn,
it's no big deal to peel away
layers of fancy robes and make
a few adjustments to the human form –
pruning some parts, enhancing others –
to produce a convincing image
of a female pope.

But it's also possible, given the long line
of St Peter's surrogate sons, plus a human
propensity for subterfuge and play,
that one woman, let's call her Joan,
might have pulled wool over Vatican eyes
to become an interesting, if unique, pontiff.

And so the mediaeval story goes.
But clearly someone was party to
her secret, even knew her hidden
places well enough to sow a seed
with the potential to become a contender
for a claim to miraculous conception.

If there's any truth in this strange tale,
there was no happy-ever-after ending
as all became unravelled when Joan
went into labour and gave birth in public
during a procession, with the consequence
that the mother – and possibly the child,
though naturally not the father –
was immediately stoned to death.

Jane Austen's tombstone

Winchester Cathedral

It is a truth
        that she was one of our greatest writers
        and that when she died it was more or less
universally acknowledged
        that a woman should be commemorated
        by who her father was, not who she was
        or what she did. On the other hand
        it was generally accepted
that a single man in possession of a good fortune
        was master of the universe
        and as a benefactor of the Church
        had a voice that was heard
        and a will that was obeyed.
        In other words, the assumption was that a woman
must be in want of
        a man to validate her as a person
        and that her only contribution
        to society was in the role of
a wife.

Point of Grace

It's one thing to be the daughter of a lighthouse keeper,
learn to row and swim, watch out for those in danger;
another to abandon safety and launch the rowing boat
on a cold, dark, stormy night.

It's one thing to look through storm-sprayed windows
and witness in stupefied horror the tragedy of shipwreck;
it's another to set out across the billows,
rowing with all one's strength to rescue possible survivors.

It's one thing to be a passenger as someone else
rows the boat through the crash and whirl of waves;
it's another to hold the boat steady while broken bodies
try desperately to clamber from the hungry rocks.

Few of us could show such heroism, overcome all trace
of fearful self-preservation; but that's the point about grace,
darling.

*Grace Darling, daughter of the Longstone Lighthouse keeper in
Northumberland, is remembered for having rowed out to rescue
survivors of a shipwreck on the rocky outcrop, Big Harcar, in
1838*

RP RIP

Rosa Parks

Contrary to the popular stories, you were not
particularly exhausted from a long day's work,
or even from carrying too much shopping;
but just tired of injustice and of giving in.

A determination you'd never felt before
covered your body like a quilt on a winter's night.
It was a black and white case of breaking the rules,
followed by unexpected consequences.

Like David with his little stone
you found to your surprise
that though you felt so insignificant,
you weren't alone, for thousands more arose

to join the boycott that would stop
the buses, not for one night, or a week,
but for three hundred and eighty one days,
bringing a giant corporation staggering to its knees.

Mother of freedom, who would have thought
you'd lie in state on Capitol Hill?
Against the odds, your disobedience
shifted the axis of the world,

reminding us that sitting still
was once the cause of a great movement,
and breaking rules can sometimes change
the course of history.

Pebbles at Hallsands

Elizabeth Prettijohn

As the sea fret cleared,
the desolation on the beach
appeared, now softly bathed
in all the innocent pastel shades
of a Victorian watercolour,

while the night of danger drifted
or was dragged back to the waves,
past sea caves where stray seals
continue to weep salty tears
in solitude.

But still the shifting pebbles sweep
along the shore, grinding their teeth
in anger while I mutter
constant curses on the dredgers
who stole our shingle bank away.

Our whole village gone, along
with all the grains of sand
we thought were infinite;
the butcher, baker and the working
pony; pet cats that chased the rats
and ran away from dogs;
the neighbour who was never
lonely and the local children
who ran and played
and swam —

All gone
sucked out to sea
or seeking solace

in the safety of the land;
all gone except for me;
and I will hold this stony outcrop
in solitary bitterness
until salt water bleaches
my bones white,
tell the story to the gulls and fulmars,
spread my indignation like a cormorant's wings
drying in the relentless winds
of history.

Whale

At last, a sighting,
far out in the vastness of the South Atlantic,
moving majestically through salt and storm
towards a circular horizon
where all the cold and troubled sea
spills into leaden sky.

Unseen for months or years,
she carries the wild
in warm pulsating blood;
revealed only when spouting
untamed triumphant poetry
high into empty air.

Paired for life
until the fateful harpoon finds its target,
piercing her mate while she is spared
to swim on through unending waves alone;
filling the empty space, the gaping hole
where water parts. What can I share

with a life so unimaginably huge?
– a vulnerability to wounds,
red blood that drains a life away,
the joyous instinct
that nurses the fruit of our bodies
with the tenderness of milk.

BIOGRAPHY – ALWYN MARRIAGE

Alwyn Marriage is widely published in magazines, anthologies and on-line, and her fourteen published books include poetry, fiction and non-fiction. She lectured in philosophy at the University of Surrey and edited a journal before being head-hunted to be Chief Executive of two international literacy and literature aid agencies. She was awarded an international Rockefeller scholarship to work on one of her non-fiction books. She has a PhD in Aesthetics, and an MSc in Environmental Architecture and Advanced Energy Studies.

After one of her poetry collections was published, and another commissioned, by Oversteps Books, she was invited to take over as Managing Editor when the previous Editor became ill; and she has run this poetry publishing house successfully since 2008. She is a research fellow at Surrey University, has held Poet in Residence posts with Ballet Rambert and Winchester Arts Festival and has won several prizes for her work. She gives frequent guest lectures and poetry readings all over Britain, Europe, Australia and New Zealand, and greatly enjoys interacting with live audiences.

Alwyn serves on the Society of Authors Poetry and Spoken Word Group committee. She is a member of Poets for the Planet and played an active part in their Twitter campaign, #BeginAfresh. She has belonged to the Poetry Society for many years, and is a member of the Devon Company of Poets and Moor Poets. Her most recent poetry collections are *In the image: Portraits of Mediaeval Women* (Indigo Dreams 2017) and *Pandora's Pandemic* (SPM Publications 2021); and her recent novels are *Rapeseed*, (Stairwell Books, 2017) and *The Elder Race* (Bellhouse Books, 2020).

More details can be found at www.marriages.me.uk.

PALEWELL PRESS

Palewell Press is an independent publisher handling poetry, fiction and non-fiction with a focus on books that foster Justice, Equality and Sustainability.

The Editor can be reached on enquiries@palewellpress.co.uk

oil
anchovy
squashed garlic, chilli flakes
cook add,
chopped stalks, chard.
chard leaves last

Pasta, cooked, use a little water
cheese